Lively Little Quilt Blocks

26 Step-by-Step Patterns

*by Joyce Libal and the Editors
of Miniature Quilts magazine*

CHITRA PUBLICATIONS

Your Best Value in Quilting

Chitra Publications
2 Public Avenue
Montrose, Pennsylvania 18801-1220

First Printing: 2000

Library of Congress Cataloging-in-Publication Data

Libal, Joyce.
    Lively little quilt blocks : 26 step-by-step patterns / by Joyce Libal and the editors of
Miniature quilts magazine.
        p. cm.
    ISBN 1-885588-33-X (pbk.)
    1. Patchwork--Patterns. 2. Miniature quilts. I. Miniature quilts. II. Title.

TT835.L48497 2000
746.46'041--dc21

00-031420

Edited by: Deborah Hearn
Design and Illustrations: Diane M. Albeck-Grick
Photography: Van Zandbergen Photography, Brackney, Pennsylvania

Our Mission Statement:

*We publish quality quilting magazines and books
that recognize, promote and inspire self-expression.
We are dedicated to serving our customers
with respect, kindness and efficiency.*

Dedication

This book is dedicated to all of the faithful readers of *Miniature Quilts* magazine who loved the "Mini Quilt Blocks A to Z" feature and requested we make it into a book.

Table of Contents

Introduction

Welcome to *Lively Little Quilt Blocks*. The idea for this book took root back in 1995, when the editors of *Miniature Quilts* magazine decided to publish the first installment of a series they called "Mini Quilt Blocks A to Z." Beginning in Issue 17 with a block called Aircraft, the magazine published a pattern for a 4 inch pieced traditional block, with a name beginning with each letter of the alphabet, in 26 consecutive issues. The series was completed in 1999 with the publication of the Z block in Issue 42. As soon as that issue hit the newsstands, readers began requesting a book containing the series.

The original patterns in the series were published in black and white and featured only diagrams of the blocks. I volunteered to make all 26 of the blocks for this book.

I didn't realize how much fun it would be to watch the little blocks materialize as I stitched. The step-by-step directions were easy to follow, and I experienced a real sense of satisfaction as each block was completed. I'm the kind of quilter who loves fabric and hates to throw the last remaining scraps away. That's why I thoroughly enjoyed showcasing some of my favorite leftovers in these delightful blocks.

I hope you'll enjoy reading the historical information that accompanies each pattern. Quilting dates back to the earliest history of the United States, and exactly when many of our traditional quilt blocks first appeared remains unknown. The earliest recorded sources of each block presented in this book are listed, however, along with many of the names that each block is known by.

As interesting as it is to read about the history surrounding some of our traditional quilt blocks, it's even more fun to make them. After stitching the 26 blocks showcased in *Lively Little Quilt Blocks*, I couldn't stop! I made a sampler with them and went on to complete the other quilts shown on the back cover. The same thing is sure to happen to you! Ideas for settings accompany the patterns, but you'll find yourself coming up with other must-stitch quilting ideas as you make these charming blocks. So, let the fun begin. Just turn the page, and watch these little blocks work their magic.

Joyce Libal

Joyce Libal
Senior Editor, *Miniature Quilts* magazine

The editorial team, clockwise from the top, Jack Braunstein, Debra Feece, Deborah Hearn, Elsie Campbell and Joyce Libal

"A" is for Aircraft

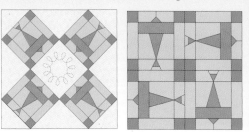

Quilters have long chosen block patterns that reflect the times in which they live. The Wright Brothers' first heavier-than-air craft flight took place in 1903 at Kittyhawk, North Carolina. Twenty-four years later, Charles Lindbergh made aviation history with his famous nonstop transatlantic flight from New York City to Paris. And in 1929, Pan American became the first international airline operation. Quilting took flight in the same year with The Aircraft Quilt block pattern from the *Kansas City Star* according to the *Encyclopedia of Pieced Quilt Patterns*. The design commemorated a form of transportation unknown at the turn of the century. Stitch a squadron of these blocks and take off with your own design for a little Aircraft quilt.

CUTTING
- Cut 1: A, light
- Cut 1: AR, same light
- Cut 2: 1 1/4" x 3" rectangles, same light
- Cut 1: D, same light
- Cut 1: DR, same light
- Cut 1: F, same light
- Cut 1: G, same light
- Cut 1: GR, same light
- Cut 4: 1 1/4" squares, medium
- Cut 1: B, dark
- Cut 1: 1 1/4" x 3" rectangle, same dark
- Cut 1: C, same dark
- Cut 1: E, same dark

DIRECTIONS
- Stitch the A and AR to adjacent sides of the B. This is the nose section.

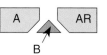

- Stitch a 1 1/4" medium square to each short end of the nose section.

- Stitch the G and GR to adjacent sides of the C. This is the body of the plane.

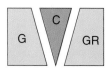

- Stitch the 1 1/4" x 3" dark rectangle to the top of the body, as shown. Stitch the 1 1/4" x 3" light rectangles to the left and right sides.

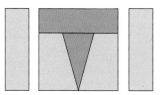

- Join the E and F, as shown. Stitch the D and DR to opposite sides. This is the tail section.

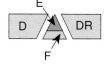

- Stitch a 1 1/4" medium square to each end of the tail section.

- Join the 3 sections to complete the block.

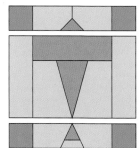

Patterns for Aircraft

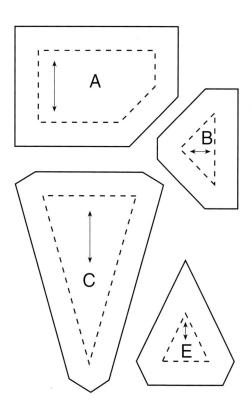

4

"B" is for Beacon Light

Begin with a center Nine Patch and add three-piece corner units for an easy-to-stitch block with lots of design potential. Choose bold colors for the cross that's formed by the triangles, arrange the blocks in a straight set and you'll get strong horizontal and vertical lines in your quilt top. Place the blocks on point, alternate them with plain blocks and let the Nine Patch shine. It's a great block for a scrappy quilt.

According to the *Encyclopedia of Pieced Quilt Patterns, Volume 1*, the block is also referred to as Union Square and was a "Nancy Cabot" pattern that appeared in the 1930s. The same pattern was also offered by *Progressive Farmer* magazine.

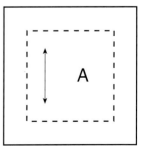

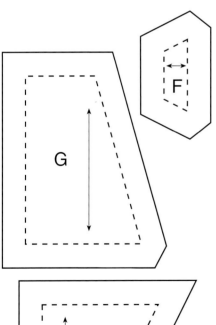

CUTTING
For each block:
- Cut 5: A, light
- Cut 4: 1 1/2" squares, light
- Cut 4: A, dark
- Cut 4: 1 7/8" squares, dark, then cut them in half diagonally to yield 8 triangles

DIRECTIONS
- Stitch light A's to 2 opposite sides of a dark A. Make 2.

- Stitch dark A's to 2 opposite sides of a light A.
- Join the three rows to complete the center Nine Patch.

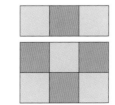

- Stitch triangles to adjacent sides of a 1 1/2" light square to make a corner unit, as shown. Press seams toward the square. Make 4.

- Stitch corner units to 2 opposite sides of the center Nine Patch. Press seams toward the center unit. Stitch corner units to the remaining sides to complete the block.

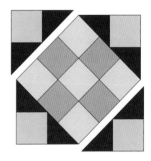

Pattern for Beacon Light

A

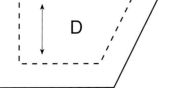

5

"C" is for Cups and Saucers

The cups and saucers block appeared in a mid-1930s issue of the *Kansas City Star* according to the *Encyclopedia of Pieced Quilt Patterns, Volume 1*. The arrangement of the small triangles creates movement in the block. Notice how your eyes move in a diagonal direction in the multi-block arrangement showing the blocks set on point. Your fabric and color choices can enhance the movement and really make the block sparkle.

Several blocks are shown set straight in the alternate arrangement in which a strong secondary pattern emerges. The dark background triangles form a stable base in which the lighter ones appear to spin.

Although the Cups and Saucers block looks complex, its construction is quite simple.

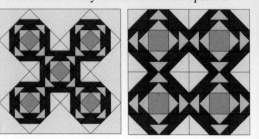

CUTTING
- Cut 4: B, light
- Cut 8: C, medium
- Cut 1: A, dark
- Cut 4: B, second dark
- Cut 16: D, same second dark

DIRECTIONS
- Stitch a second dark B to a light B to make a pieced square. Make 4.
- Stitch D's to opposite sides of a C to form a Flying Geese unit. Make 8.

- Join two Flying Geese units, as shown. Make 4.

- Lay out the 4 pieced squares, 4 Flying Geese units and the A. Stitch the units into rows, as shown, and join the rows to complete the block.

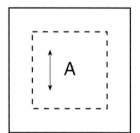

Patterns for Cups and Saucers

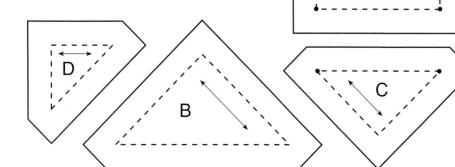

Patterns for David and Goliath

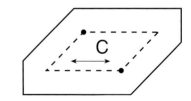

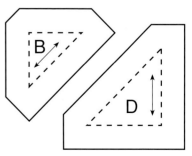

"D" is for David and Goliath

This challenging block pattern was inspired by a well-known Bible story. Ruth Finley's 1929 book, *Old Patchwork Quilts and the Women Who Made Them*, describes the block as "being reminiscent of David's sling-shot of accurate aim." Other names for the block include The Four Darts, The Bull's Eye, Flying Darts and Doe and Darts.

Experiment with color and the placement of light, medium and dark fabrics in the block. It's interesting to see how the look changes as you move the values around.

This block is a good candidate for using a striped fabric in selected A and C positions, as seen in the sample block. By controlling the direction of the stripe, you can achieve interesting movement in the design.

Notice the strong interlocking design formed by the A and C pieces that emerges when the blocks are straight set. You might also add interest by using a variety of scraps for the secondary Four Patch formed by the corner A pieces.

The blocks take on a more delicate, less complex look when set on point with plain alternate blocks. Or combine David and Goliath blocks with another pieced pattern such as the Hour Glass. Have some design fun with this fascinating block.

CUTTING
- Cut 8: A, light
- Cut 8: B, same light
- Cut 4: A, medium
- Cut 4: C, same medium
- Cut 4: CR, same medium
- Cut 1: A, dark
- Cut 4: C, same dark
- Cut 4: CR, same dark
- Cut 4: D, same dark

DIRECTIONS
- Stitch a light A to a medium A, to make a pieced rectangle. Make 4.
- Stitch a dark CR to a medium C, as shown, backstitching at the dot.
- Set in a light B triangle. Make 4. Set them aside.

- In the same manner, stitch a meduim CR to a dark C. Set in a light B triangle, as before. Make 4.
- Stitch a remaining light A square to the dark C in one of these units, backstitching 1/4" from the edge, as shown. Make 4.

- Stitch one of the units you set aside to the adjacent side of the square in the same manner, as shown.

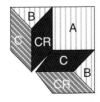

- Align the diagonal edges of the dark C and dark CR. Stitch from the outside edge to the dot and backstitch.

- Stitch a dark D triangle to the unit to complete a corner unit, as shown. Make 4.

- Lay out the corner units, the pieced rectangles and the dark A, as shown. Stitch them into rows and join the rows to complete the block.

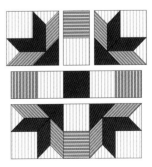

"E" is for Eight Point Design

Eight Point Design is a popular block that is also known by more than a dozen other names, some of which have resulted from slight variations in the number of fabrics used and their placement.

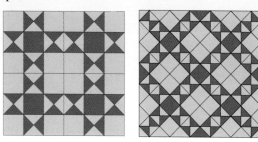

Mosaic   Ohio Star   Variable Star   Flying Crow

You'll need only two fabrics to piece this block, but see how lively those two fabrics can look in both a straight and on-point set.

The design lends itself to a scrappy look too. What if you cut the center square to include an interesting motif from a preprint or a tiny plaid that resembles a pieced Nine Patch? Imagine using holiday fabric for a seasonal touch. Have fun stitching your blocks into your own one-of-a-kind quilt.

CUTTING
- Cut 4: A, light
- Cut 8: B, same light
- Cut 1: A, dark
- Cut 8: B, same dark

DIRECTIONS
- Stitch a dark B to a light B along one short side to make a pieced triangle, as shown. Make 8.

- Stitch a pair of pieced triangles together, as shown, to complete a pieced square. Make 4.

- Lay out all the pieces, as shown. Stitch the pieces into rows and join the rows to complete the block.

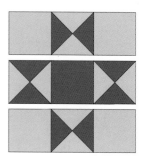

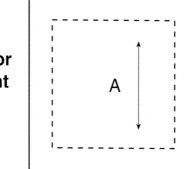

Patterns for Eight Point Design

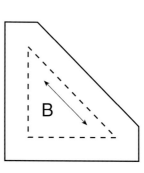

"F" is for Forest Paths

The Forest Paths block was offered by the *Farm Journal* and is classified as a "block with unpieced corners" according to Barbara Brackman's *Encyclopedia of Pieced Quilt Patterns*.

Place the darkest and lightest values in the pieced squares in the center of the block. The more contrast you achieve there, the more apparent the pinwheel will be when you set the blocks together. When Forest Paths blocks are joined in a straight set, the Four Patch where the corners meet becomes an inviting spot to play with color and fabrics, especially if you're using scraps. Join them in an on-point setting, or combine them with other 4" blocks in a setting of your choice to create your own unique quilt design.

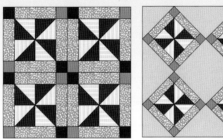

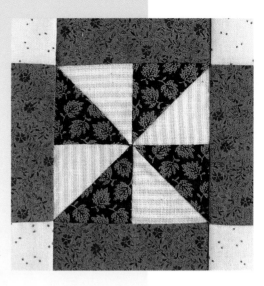

CUTTING
- Cut 2: 2 1/8" squares, light
- Cut 4: 1 1/4" squares, light
- Cut 4: 1 1/4" x 3" strips, medium
- Cut 2: 2 1/8" squares, dark

DIRECTIONS
- Draw a diagonal line from corner to corner on the wrong side of each 2 1/8" light square, as shown.

- Place a marked light square on a 2 1/8" dark square, right sides together. Stitch 1/4" away from the diagonal line on both sides, as shown. Make 2.

- Cut the squares on the drawn line to yield 4 pieced squares.

- Stitch two pieced squares together, as shown. Make 2.

- Join the pieced units to form a pinwheel, as shown.

- Stitch 1 1/4" x 3" medium strips to 2 opposite sides of the pinwheel.

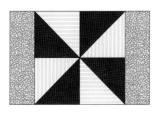

- Stitch a 1 1/4" light square to each short end of a remaining 1 1/4" x 3" medium strip to make a pieced strip. Make 2.

- Stitch the pieced strips to the remaining sides of the pinwheel unit to complete the block.

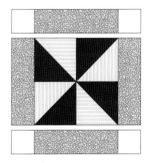

"G" is for Going to Chicago

The Going to Chicago block is attributed to Nancy Page and was inspired by an event important in both world history and quilt history—the international exhibition known as A Century of Progress Exposition. Planned to showcase cultural and commercial products of participating nations, this ninth World's Fair was held near Chicago from 1933 to 1934. The fair emphasized scientific exhibits and attracted more than 40 million visitors. It was the first of the World's Fairs to show a profit despite its being held during the depression era.

The renowned quilting contest sponsored by Sears Roebuck and Co. culminated in the awarding of a $1,200 grand prize and an exhibit of regional prizewinners. It was enormously successful, attracting more than 24,000 entries.

According to the *Encyclopedia of Pieced Quilt Patterns*, the block is also known by seven other names including World's Fair, New Four Patch, Jacob's Ladder, Railroad and Buckeye Beauty.

Regardless of what you call it, the block is easy to piece. The strong diagonal direction of the block is enhanced when several blocks are set straight. Setting them on point emphasizes the vertical direction. Look at what happens when you change directions and some of the blocks go east while some go west! Can you see the Variable Star emerging as a secondary design?

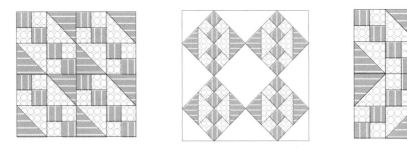

CUTTING
- Cut 4: 1 1/2" squares, light
- Cut 1: 2 7/8" square, same light,
- Cut 4: 1 1/2" squares, medium
- Cut 1: 2 7/8" square, same medium

DIRECTIONS
- Stitch a 1 1/2" light square to a 1 1/2" medium square. Make 4.

- Stitch 2 units together to make a Four Patch. Make 2.

- Draw a diagonal line from corner to corner on the wrong side of the 2 7/8" light square.

- Place the marked light square on the 2 7/8" medium square, right sides together. Stitch 1/4" away from the diagonal line on both sides, as shown.

- Cut the square on the drawn line to yield 2 pieced squares.
- Lay out the units, as shown. Stitch them into pairs and join the pairs to complete the block.

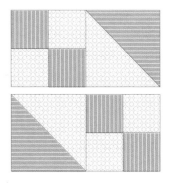

"H" is for Henry of the West

"Of political names given quilts by their makers there were scores," wrote Ruth Finley in *Old Patchwork Quilts and The Women Who Made Them*. One such block is Henry of the West, named in honor of the "Great Pacificator," Henry Clay. As a Representative and later a Senator, Clay is known as a sponsor of such legislation on slavery issues as the Missouri Compromise and the Compromise of 1850. The Kentucky politician ran unsuccessfully for the US Presidency in 1824, 1832 and 1844 but continued to serve in Congress until 1848, just two years before his death.

Ms. Finley's book also refers to the block as Clay's Choice, Harry's Star and Star of the West. The *Encyclopedia of Pieced Quilt Patterns* lists three other names for the block including Clay's Star, a mail-order pattern from The McKim Studio, and Beauty Patch, published by the Old Chelsea Station Needlecraft Service. The "Nancy Cabot" column featured the block as Clay's Favorite.

Set straight, the blocks create secondary Four Patches at the corners and this could invite some interesting color play. Equally interesting are the results of rearranging the placement of light, medium and dark values. What if you combined a mixture of these light and dark blocks in the same quilt? See what they look like sashed or set alternately with other blocks from this book, or combine them with simple Four Patch blocks.

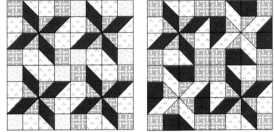

CUTTING
- Cut 8: 1 1/2" squares, light
- Cut 8: 1 1/2" squares, medium
- Cut 4: 1 1/2" x 2 1/2" rectangles, dark

DIRECTIONS
- Lay a 1 1/2" medium square on the one end of a 1 1/2" x 2 1/2" dark rectangle. Stitch a diagonal line, from corner to corner, as shown.

- Trim 1/4" beyond the stitched line and press the unit open.

- In the same manner, place, stitch and trim a 1 1/2" light square to the opposite end, as shown, to make pieced rectangle A. Make 4.

- Stitch a 1 1/2" light square to a 1 1/2" medium square to make pieced rectangle B, as shown. Make 4.

- Stitch a pieced rectangle A to a pieced rectangle B, as shown, to make a pieced square. Make 4.

- Lay out the pieced squares, as shown. Stitch them into pairs and join the pairs to complete the block.

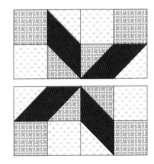

"I" is for Interwoven

Now here's a Nine Patch with personality! The Interwoven block was once featured in the Nancy Page syndicated column. According to the *Encyclopedia of Pieced Quilt Patterns*, the block was also known as Strips and Squares, Hand Weave, Handwoven and Over and Under. "Nancy Cabot" published the block in 1934, calling it Handcraft.

Set straight, you have an opportunity to emphasize the lattice look of the block. You might select fabrics for these pieces that will achieve a three-dimensional look. Secondary Four Patches are created at the corners when blocks are set this way.

When placed on point, you can emphasize the chevrons that are formed. Imagine using a floral print in all of the squares and the larger rectangles with a superimposed lattice created by the A pieces. In either setting, the center square piece looks framed. For fun, try centering a preprint fabric motif there.

CUTTING
- Cut 4: A, light
- Cut 4: AR, same light
- Cut 1: 1 3/4" square, same light
- Cut 4: 1 3/8" squares, medium
- Cut 4: 1" x 1 3/4" rectangles, same medium
- Cut 4: 1 3/8" x 1 3/4" rectangles, dark

DIRECTIONS
- Stitch a 1 3/8" square to an A, stopping and backstitching 1/4" from the edge of the square, as shown.

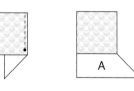

- In the same manner, stitch an AR to the adjacent side of the square.

- Align the diagonal edges of the A and AR. Stitch from the outside edge to the dot and backstitch to complete a corner unit. Make 4.

- Stitch a 1" x 1 3/4" medium rectangle to a 1 3/8" x 1 3/4" dark rectangle, right

sides together along their length, to complete a side unit. Make 4.

- Lay out the 1 3/4" center square and pieced units. Stitch the units into rows and join the rows to complete the block.

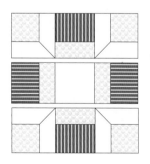

Pattern for Interwoven

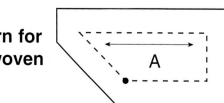

"J" is for Jack in the Box

Like the children's toy it was probably named after, Jack in the Box has plenty of movement. The McKim Studios originally published the block which is also identified as Whirligig in Carrie A. Hall and Rose G. Kretsinger's *The Romance of the Patchwork Quilt*. The "Nancy Cabot" column called the block Wheel of Fortune and Wheel of Chance.

Slight variations in piecing account for some of the different names. You can piece it using four Flying Geese units, four pieced rectangles, four rectangles and a square.

You can also stitch it as I've done using 16 pieced squares, four rectangles and a square.

Try emphasizing various parts of the block with color or prints. Use a warm color such as bright red for the rectangles and a cool color such as deep green for the pieced squares. You'll create a block with a festive holiday look and achieve depth in design. How would the block change if you reversed the placement of the warm and cool colors? Designing with these blocks can be fun, whether you set them straight or on point.

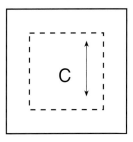

CUTTING

- Cut 16: A, light
- Cut 1: C, light
- Cut 16: A, dark
- Cut 4: B, dark

DIRECTIONS

- Stitch a dark A to a light A to make a pieced square. Make 16.

- Lay out 4 pieced squares and stitch them together to make a pieced unit, as shown. Make 4.

- Lay out 2 pieced units and a B and stitch them together to make a pieced row, as shown. Make 2.

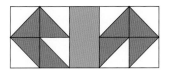

- Stitch a C between two B's to make the center row.

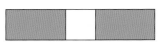

- Lay out the rows and join them to complete the block.

Patterns for Jack in the Box

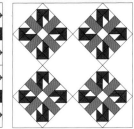

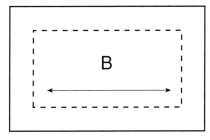

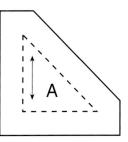

"K" is for Key West Beauty

Both a cross and a star are formed within the Key West Beauty block. It differs from the well-known Kaleidoscope pattern in that the triangles separating the arms of the cross are pieced, forming the secondary star design. Categorized as a Maltese Cross in the *Encyclopedia of Pieced Quilt Patterns*, the block is divided into eight sections by diagonal seams. Key West Beauty was published in the 1920s by the Ladies Art Company. The design is also known as Dakota Star and was published under that name in *Hearth and Home*, a Maine periodical that also offered mail-order patterns.

Piecing variations create similar yet entirely different blocks such as Key West Star, in which the corner section is left unpieced. In another *Hearth and Home* design known as Concord, the corner section is composed of three pieces.

Key West Star   Concord

This is a fun block for experimenting with directional prints such as stripes or plaids. Try placing the lines in the cross (A pieces) vertically or horizontally to add movement to the block. Use color to achieve special effects. Cut the star (C pieces) from a deep jewel tone or even black for depth. Then use a bright fabric such as fuchsia for the cross. It will advance to dance on the surface of the block, creating a lively look. Imagine how the block might look if you selected the same light fabric for the B and D pieces. The block is somewhat busy because of the many seams, so you may find that solid fabrics or those with small scale prints work best.

Notice the secondary Four Patch diamond created when the blocks are set together. Again, because of the many seamlines and points, there are several places where careful matching is required when joining the blocks. You may wish to cut sashing strips to separate them and make construction a bit easier. Notice how setting them on point emphasizes the Maltese Cross design.

CUTTING
- Cut 8: D, light
- Cut 4: A, medium
- Cut 4: B, dark
- Cut 4: C, dark

DIRECTIONS
- Stitch a medium A to a dark B to make a pieced kite unit, as shown. Make 4.
- Lay out 2 light D's and a dark C and stitch them together to make a pieced triangle, as shown. Make 4.

- Lay out 2 pieced kite units and 2 pieced triangles and join them to complete a half block, as shown. Repeat with the remaining units.

- Join the half blocks to complete the block.

Patterns for Key West Beauty

(Patterns continued on page 23)

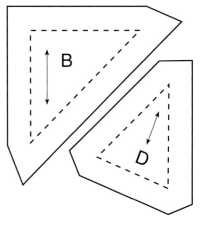

"L" is for Lincoln's Platform

Quilt block names were frequently derived from political figures and events. As a result of the Lincoln-Douglas debates in 1858, Abraham Lincoln became nationally known for his oratory skills and his opposition to the expansion of slavery in US territories. The debates were held during the senatorial campaigns of Illinois candidates Lincoln and the incumbent Senator Stephen A. Douglas. Although Lincoln lost that election, it was just two years later that he was elected President of the United States.

According to the *Encyclopedia of Pieced Quilt Patterns*, the block was among the earliest patterns available from the Ladies Art Company, perhaps as early as 1889. A variation of the block is known as Abe Lincoln's Platform.

Although depicted in most sources as a two-color block, you may wish to apply the principle of value by using a darker fabric for the pieced squares. This can enhance the Shoo Fly design in the center. You might also use scraps for the light and dark squares that frame the Shoo Fly to add interest to the block.

Because there are seven equal divisions along each edge, setting the blocks straight means matching many seams. You may find joining the blocks with sashing strips is an easier construction method. Their use will also provide a resting place for the eye between blocks. Setting the blocks on point with alternate squares will also eliminate the need to match seams.

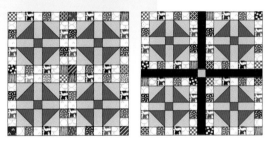

CUTTING
- Cut 4: A, light
- Cut 12: B, light
- Cut 4: C, light; or cut two 2" squares, then cut them in half diagonally
- Cut 13: B, dark
- Cut 4: C, dark; or cut two 2" squares, then cut them in half diagonally

DIRECTIONS
- Stitch a light triangle to a dark triangle to make a pieced square. Make 4.

- Stitch a light A between 2 pieced squares to form a pieced rectangle, as shown. Make 2.

- Stitch a dark B between 2 light A's to form a pieced row.

- Stitch the pieced row between the pieced rectangles to complete the block center.

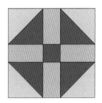

- Lay out 3 light B's and 2 dark B's and join them to make a pieced row, as shown. Make 4.

- Stitch a pieced row to each of 2 opposite sides of the block center.

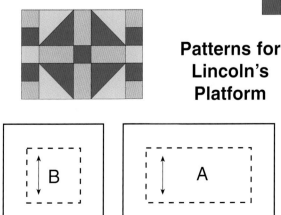

- Stitch a dark B to each end of the remaining pieced rows and stitch them to the remaining sides of the block center to complete the block.

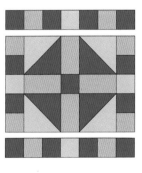

Patterns for Lincoln's Platform

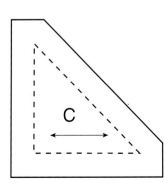

15

"M" is for Maud's Album Block

The idea that every quilt tells a story is never more true than in a signature or album quilt. A search of pattern sources reveals dozens of pieced block patterns used in album quilts. One such block is Maud's Album Block, a Nancy Page design. As with many patterns, Maud's Album Block is also known by other names. According to the *Encyclopedia of Pieced Quilt Patterns*, it was called The Mountain Peak in the *Kansas City Star*, and Old Italian Design in the *Farm Journal*. The Ladies Art Company called the block Snowflake and it was also known as Cross Stitch and Snow Block, both "Nancy Cabot" designs.

While the block is easy to piece, straight setting several of them may be a challenge because of their diagonal orientation. Notice the number of match points when four blocks are set this way. You may prefer to use narrow sashing strips between the blocks. The sashing not only breaks up the long diagonal lines, but also is forgiving of slight variations in piecing.

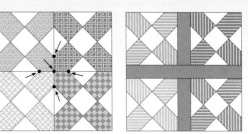

The block lends itself to a scrappy look. Imagine the added interest and movement you would gain by cutting the corner A's from plaids, checks or stripes. Make a special memory quilt by recording the signatures and sayings of family and friends in Maud's Album blocks.

CUTTING
- Cut 4: B, white
- Cut 1: C, white
- Cut 4: A, medium print

DIRECTIONS
- Stitch B's to opposite sides of an A to make a corner section, as shown. Make 2.

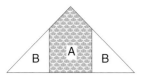

- Stitch A's to opposite sides of the C to make the center row.

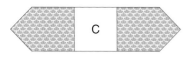

- Stitch the center row between the corner sections to complete the block.

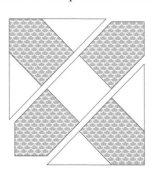

Patterns for Maud's Album Block

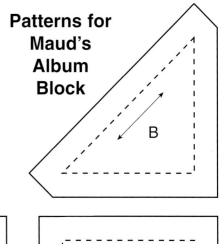

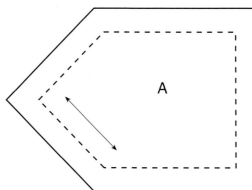

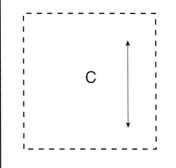

"N" is for Nonsense

This two-color block is known by several names. First published in the late 19th century by the Ladies Art Company, the block was called Boy's Nonsense. Later, when the St. Louis mail-order pattern company published a revised catalog of quilt patterns, the block was simply called Nonsense. The same pattern was published under the name Boy's Fancy in the early 1930s by *The Rural New Yorker*, a periodical, and as Boy's Playmate in the "Nancy Cabot" column.

The rather large, unbroken rectangles and square provide a place to show off some of your favorite fabrics. Imagine the block pieced using plaids for a country look. Or achieve a vintage look with reproduction '30s prints. Even some large-scale prints will work nicely in the center square and rectangles. What if you reversed the placement of light and dark values in the block?

Set straight, the block has a diagonal look because of the predominant diagonal seams and the square-in-a-square center. Notice how placing it on point actually creates a boxier look. That's because those diagonal seams are now positioned so that vertical and horizontal lines receive emphasis.

Although the traditional pattern is pieced using two fabrics, why not take some creative license and stitch it with more? Add movement with stripe fabrics or add a touch of whimsy by centering a novelty print in the square. Sew a little Nonsense today!

CUTTING
- Cut 8: A, light
- Cut 2: 2 3/8" squares, same light, then cut them in half diagonally to yield 4 large triangles
- Cut 4: B, dark
- Cut 1: 1 7/8" square, dark

DIRECTIONS
- Stitch A's to 2 opposite sides of the dark square.
- Stitch 2 A's to the remaining sides, as shown, to complete the square-in-a-square.

- Stitch a large light triangle to a dark B along their long sides to make a corner section. Make 2.
- Stitch the corner sections to opposite sides of the square-in-a-square to com-

plete the block center, as shown.

- Stitch an A to each short end of a remaining dark B. Stitch a large light triangle to a long side of the B, as shown, to complete a corner unit. Make 2.

- Stitch the corner units to opposite sides of the block center to complete the block.

Patterns for Nonsense

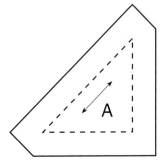

17

"O" is for Old Maid's Puzzle

What could be simpler than this Four Patch block? First published in the mid-1930s, the design is attributed to "Nancy Cabot." A host of similar blocks known by other names can be created by making small changes in coloring or piecing. For example, cutting the triangles and two of the squares from the same fabric results in a block known as Anvil. Rotating the sections with the small pieced squares yields a block named Fox and Geese.

An earlier design also known as Old Maid's Puzzle was published by the Ladies Art Company.

Because the block has a diagonal orientation, it can give your quilt a dynamic look. See what happens when four blocks are set straight but their direction is alternated. Notice the secondary star design that appears in the first arrangement. Imagine a scrappy look for either of them. Or, consider piecing blocks in which the value placement is reversed, creating dark and light blocks. Then combine them in a quilt for an effective design. There's no doubt you're in for some design fun with this easy-to-sew block.

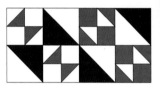

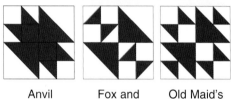

| Anvil | Fox and Geese | Old Maid's Puzzle, Ladies Art Company |

CUTTING
- Cut 1: 2 7/8" square, light
- Cut 2: 1 7/8" squares, light
- Cut 4: 1 1/2" squares, light
- Cut 1: 2 7/8" square, medium
- Cut 2: 1 7/8" squares, dark

DIRECTIONS
- Draw a diagonal line from corner to corner on the wrong side of each 1 7/8" light square, as shown.

- Draw a diagonal line from corner to corner on the wrong side of the 2 7/8" light square.

- Lay a marked 1 7/8" light square on a 1 7/8" dark square, right sides together.
- Stitch 1/4" away from the drawn line on both sides, as shown. Make 2.

- Cut the squares on the drawn line to yield 4 small pieced squares.
- Lay the marked 2 7/8" light square on the 2 7/8" medium square, right sides together.
- Stitch 1/4" away from the drawn line on both sides.
- Cut the square on the drawn line to yield 2 large pieced squares.
- Lay out two 1 1/2" light squares and 2 small pieced squares, as shown. Stitch

them into pairs and join the pairs to make a Four Patch. Make 2.

- Lay out the Four Patches and the large pieced squares, as shown. Stitch the units into pairs and join the pairs to complete the block.

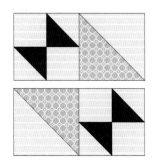

"P" is for Patch Blossom

In the *Encyclopedia of Pieced Quilt Patterns* compiled by Barbara Brackman, Patch Blossom, an Aunt Martha design, is one of more than 40 traditional blocks categorized as "trees with triangles for leaves."

Make the Patch Blossom block to fit any season. Why not use it in a holiday quilt or sampler? Because of its realistic nature, the block may look best when placed on point. However, blocks set straight with sashing also make a pleasing arrangement.

Remember to choose small scale prints for the A pieces that make the pieced squares because large scale prints may lose their impact here.

CUTTING
- Cut 1: A, light
- Cut 2: B, same light
- Cut 10: A, medium
- Cut 15: A, dark
- Cut 2: A, brown
- Cut 1: 1 5/8" x 2 3/4" rectangle, brown

DIRECTIONS
- Stitch a medium A to a dark A to make a pieced square. Make 10.
- Stitch 4 pieced squares together. Stitch a dark A to one end to make a pieced row, as shown.

- In the same manner, stitch 3 pieced squares together and stitch a dark A to one end.
- Stitch 2 pieced squares together and a dark A to one end, as before.

- Stitch a dark A to one pieced square, as shown.

- Lay out and join the rows, as shown. Stitch a dark triangle to the pieced unit to form a half block.

- Stitch a brown A to a light B to form a branch unit. Make 2.

- Stitch the light A to one short end of the brown rectangle to form a trunk unit.

- Stitch the branch units to opposite sides of the trunk unit to form the remaining half block.

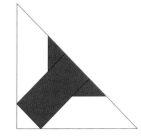

- Join the halves to complete the block.

Patterns for Patch Blossom

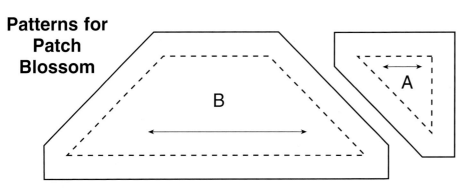

"Q" is for Quail's Nest

Does the Quail's Nest block look familiar? Perhaps you know this Nine Patch design by one of its other names, including Churn Dash, Shoo Fly, Monkey Wrench and Hole in the Barn Door. According to the *Encyclopedia of Pieced Quilt Patterns*, it was also named Quail's Nest in 1975 by a mail-order pattern source known as Mrs. Danner's Quilts.

Regardless of what you call the block, it is a simple, graphic design that is easy to piece. Your selection of fabrics and setting provide the key to creating a variety of looks. Achieve an antique look by setting two-color blocks on point. Or use homespun plaids in straight-set blocks for a country feel.

Experiment with sashing, setting and color for even more variety. Reversing the traditional placement of light and dark pieces in some of the blocks creates an interesting positive/negative look.

What if you used black with jewel-tone solids for an Amish-style quilt? You'll find this versatile block has plenty of design potential.

CUTTING
- Cut 4: A, light
- Cut 4: B, same light
- Cut 1: C, same light
- Cut 4: A, dark
- Cut 4: B, same dark

DIRECTIONS
- Stitch a light A to a dark A to make Unit 1. Make 4.

- Stitch a light B to a dark B to make Unit 2. Make 4.

- Stitch Unit 1's to two opposite sides of a Unit 2 to form a row, as shown. Make 2.

- Stitch Unit 2's to two opposite sides of the light C, as shown, to form the center row.

- Lay out the rows and join them to complete the block.

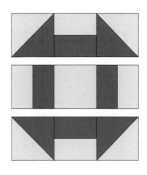

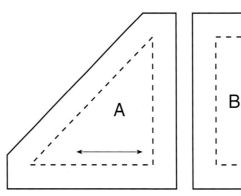

Patterns for Quail's Nest

"R" is for The Rosebud

The Rosebud block was first published by the *Kansas City Star* in 1942. According to the *Encyclopedia of Pieced Quilt Patterns*, it is categorized as an unequal Nine Patch with a large center square and squares in the corners.

Audition several fabrics for the block to determine which ones emphasize the rose-

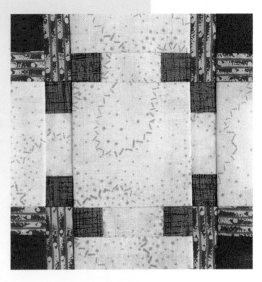

bud design most effectively. When set straight, the squares and rectangles create an overall "chain" pattern. However, because this set may cause the rosebud design to become less distinct, you may wish to separate the blocks with narrow sashing.

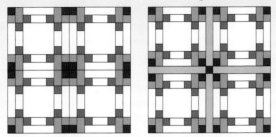

If you wish to preserve the design in a straight set without sashing, try using different shades of the same color to create the rosebuds. Using different values will allow the rosebuds to remain evident when the blocks are set side-by-side.

Placing the blocks in a diagonal set with alternate plain squares will allow you to emphasize the rosebuds. Here's where color and fabric play can really make a difference. Create a classic by using red and deep pink prints for the rosebuds, emerald green for the leaves and a crisp white-on-white print for the background. Imagine the drama of using yellow and gold prints for the rosebuds, apple green for the leaves and a deep navy tone-on-tone for the background!

Our instructions simplify the stitching by using a rectangle instead of two of the squares in the traditional corner Four Patch, thus eliminating a seam.

Stitch several blocks and have some creative fun with The Rosebud!

CUTTING
- Cut 2: 2 1/2" squares, light
- Cut 2: 1" x 2 1/2" strips, same light
- Cut 1: 1 1/2" x 4 1/2" strip, same light
- Cut 2: 1" x 4 1/2" strips, leaf print
- Cut 4: 1" x 1 1/2" strips, medium rosebud print
- Cut 2: 1" x 2 1/2" strips, medium rosebud print
- Cut 2: 1" x 2 1/2" strips, dark rosebud print

DIRECTIONS
- Stitch the 1 1/2" x 4 1/2" light strip between the 1" x 4 1/2" leaf print strips, along their length, to make a pieced strip. Cut four 1" wide slices from the pieced strip.

- Stitch a 1" x 2 1/2" light strip to a slice, along their length, to make a pieced unit. Make 2.
- Stitch them to opposite sides of a 2 1/2" light square to make the center unit.
- Stitch 1" x 1 1/2" medium rosebud print strips to both ends of the 2 remaining slices to make 2 long pieced strips.

- Stitch them to opposite sides of the center unit.

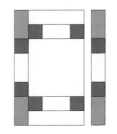

- Stitch a 1" x 2 1/2" medium rosebud print strip to a 1" x 2 1/2" dark rosebud print strip, along their length. Make 2.

- Stitch them to opposite sides of the remaining 2 1/2" light square, placing the medium rosebud print against the light square. Cut two 1"-wide slices from this pieced strip.
- Stitch them to opposite sides of the center unit to complete the block.

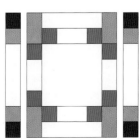

"S" is for Sugar Bowl

Sugar Bowl was published in 1927 by *Capper's Weekly*. It also appeared in the "Nancy Cabot" column and the *Farm Journal*.

Knowing the era of its first publication can give you some fabric hints for achieving a vintage look. Try piecing the blocks using muslin and Depression-era reproduction prints.

The Sugar Bowl block can be set straight or on point. Use it in a sampler with other similar Basket blocks. You may be surprised by the number of variations you'll find. Separate the straight-set blocks with sashing and cornerstones for a traditional look.

Set on point with alternating plain squares, the block looks even more realistic. Explore the impact of color on design in this arrangement. Imagine the drama of using a black or navy background with bright solids in an Amish-style palette. Searching for just the right small-scale plaids for country-style

baskets might be fun. And rich floral or paisley prints can lend a sophisticated, elegant touch to your little quilt.

CUTTING
- Cut 1: 2 7/8" square, light, then cut it in half diagonally to yield 2 large triangles
- Cut 2: 1 7/8" squares, same light
- Cut 2: 1 1/2" x 2 1/2" rectangles, same light
- Cut 1: 2 7/8" square, dark, then cut it in half diagonally to yield 2 large triangles. You will use one.
- Cut 3: 1 7/8" squares, same dark, then cut one of them in half diagonally to yield 2 small triangles
- Cut 1: 1 1/2" square, same dark

DIRECTIONS
- Draw a diagonal line from corner to corner on the wrong side of each 1 7/8" light square, as shown.
- Place a marked square on a 1 7/8" dark square, right sides together. Stitch 1/4" away from the drawn line on both sides. Make 2.
- Cut on the drawn line to yield 4 pieced squares.
- Stitch a large light triangle to a large dark triangle to form a large pieced square.
- Stitch a small dark trian-

gle to the end of a light rectangle to make a base unit. Make a second base unit, reversing the placement of the small dark triangle, as shown.

- Stitch 2 small pieced squares together, as shown.

- Stitch this unit to the large pieced square.

- Stitch the dark square and 2 small pieced squares into a row, as shown.

- Stitch this row to the large pieced square unit to complete the basket section.

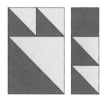

- Stitch the base units to adjacent sides of the basket section.

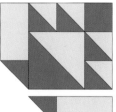

- Stitch the remaining large light triangle to the unit to complete the block.

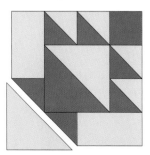

"T" is for Tam's Patch

Composed of squares and rectangles, this Four-Patch design known as Tam's Patch was first published in *The Perfect Patchwork Primer* by Beth Gutcheon. However, a similar but unnamed block pattern was available earlier as a Laura Wheeler design

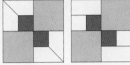

from Old Chelsea Station Needlecraft Service. Notice that the later variation is easier to piece because all of the seams are straight while the earlier block has four odd-shaped pieces that require a Y-seam.

Tam's Patch invites design and fabric play. When set straight with all of the blocks positioned the same, the small dark squares lend a directional look to the arrangement. You may wish to emphasize this by selecting fabrics with a lot of contrast. By rotating the direction of the blocks in a straight set, an interlocking design emerges at block intersections. Using a stripe or other directional fabric in the rectangles that create this secondary design could add vibrant interest to your quilt. When the blocks are set on point, the small dark squares again create a strong focus. Cut them from a single dark fabric to achieve a chain look and add color excitement by using light and

medium print scraps for the remaining pieces.

The blocks might be perfect for a pieced border. Or, create your own Tam's Patch variation by turning two sections of the block so that the dark squares are in the outside corners. It's fun to take creative license and come up with a new twist on a traditional block.

CUTTING
- Cut 2: 1 1/2" squares, light
- Cut 2: 1 1/2" x 2 1/2" rectangles, same light
- Cut 2: 2 1/2" squares, medium
- Cut 2: 1 1/2" squares, dark

DIRECTIONS
- Stitch a 1 1/2" dark square to a 1 1/2" light square to form a pieced rectangle. Make 2.
- Stitch a 1 1/2" x 2 1/2" light rectangle to a pieced rectangle to complete a section. Make 2.

- Stitch a section to a 2 1/2" medium square to make a half block, as shown. Make 2.

- Join the half blocks to complete the block.

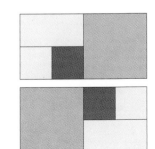

Patterns for Key West Beauty

(Patterns continued from page 14)

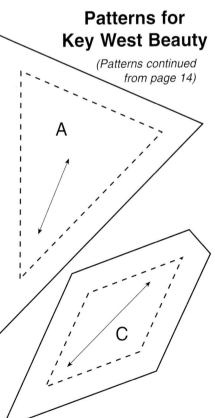

"U" is for Underground Railroad

The Underground Railroad block was first described by Ruth Finley in her book, *Old Patchwork Quilts and the Women Who Made Them*. In it, she links the pattern's name with regional history, noting that the block was called Underground Railroad in an area of the United States known as the Western Reserve (ultimately Ohio, Indiana, Illinois, Michigan and Wisconsin). Elsewhere, it was known as The Trail of the Covered Wagon (Mississippi and west) or The Trail of Benjamin's Kite (to commemorate Benjamin Franklin's famous electrical experiment in Pennsylvania).

Foot Prints
in the Sands
of Time

Blue Chains

According to the *Encyclopedia of Pieced Quilt Patterns*, this Nine Patch design has still other names including Jacob's Ladder. Simple changes in coloring result in a block named Foot Prints in the Sands of Time as published in *The Drover's Journal*. A variation called Blue Chains appeared in a 1936 "Nancy Cabot" column.

Set Underground Railroad blocks straight or on point. Notice how different a set with blocks oriented in the same direction looks from one in which the direction is alternated.

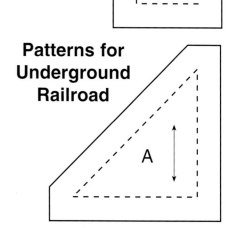

CUTTING
- Cut 4: A, light
- Cut 10: B, same light
- Cut 10: B, medium
- Cut 4: A, dark

DIRECTIONS
- Stitch a dark A to a light A to form a pieced square. Make 4.

- Stitch a medium B to a light B to form a pieced rectangle. Make 10.

- Join 2 pieced rectangles to form a Four Patch. Make 5.

- Lay out the Four Patches and pieced squares, as shown. Stitch them into rows and join the rows to complete a block.

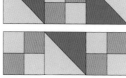

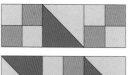

Patterns for Underground Railroad

B

A

"V" is for Virginia Snowball

Virginia Snowball appeared in *Farmer's Wife*, but other sources published the block under different names. Named Snowball, it appeared in a 1933 "Nancy Cabot" column. Kansas City's Colonial Patterns, Inc. sold an Aunt Martha pattern, calling it Four Point.

You might be surprised to learn that this block is classified as a square-in-a-square design. According to the *Encyclopedia of Pieced Quilt Patterns*, it's categorized this way because it is composed of a "squeezed" center square that is "built up into a larger square" with the addition of the curved corner shapes.

Experiment with color and value while playing with Virginia Snowball blocks. When set straight, round "snowballs" appear at the block intersections. What if you alternated dark blocks with light ones? Consider

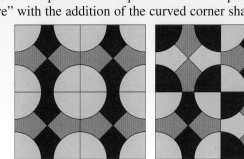

using the block as a centerpiece and continue the square-in-a-square idea by adding corner triangles to it.

In keeping with the era of the block's origin, use 1930s-style reproduction prints for the A pieces. It's a perfect pattern for the scrappy look.

CUTTING
- Cut 4: B, light
- Cut 2: A, medium
- Cut 2: A, dark

DIRECTIONS
- Stitch a dark A to a medium A, as shown. Make 2.

- Join them to make the center unit.

- Fold each light B in half and pinch to crease the mid-point of the curved side. Place a light B on one side of the center unit, right sides together, aligning the crease on the B with the seam intersection of the center unit. Place a pin at the crease.

- Align the straight edges of the B with those of the center unit and pin at each end. Place more pins to secure the pieces while you align the curved edges. Stitch, sewing slowly and easing the pieces as necessary to complete the curved seam.

- Stitch the remaining light B's to the center unit in the same manner to complete a Virginia Snowball block. Press the block from the back, directing seam allowances toward the B's and distributing fullness evenly.

Patterns for Virginia Snowball

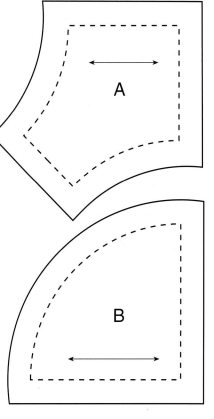

"W" is for Wheels

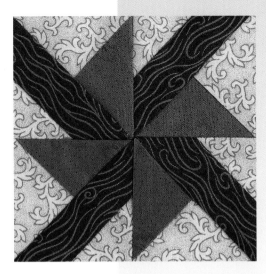

Two kinds of pieced triangles combine to make the Four Patch block known as Wheels. The good news is that you can use easy strip piecing and rotary cutting construction techniques to make it quickly. One pieced triangle is sewn from two small triangles cut from a square. The other one is cut from a pieced strip using a cutting guide.

First published in *Progressive Farmer*, the block creates a feeling of movement because of its angles and diagonal lines. Joining them side by side in a straight set can impart a busy feeling to a quilt. Therefore, you may prefer to set them together with sashing strips and cornerstones to quiet the design and provide a resting place for the eye.

Setting the blocks on point does not increase the block movement. However, it does create strong vertical and horizontal lines not evident in straight sets. Using color and value in the block can be fun. Consider reversing the value placement and making a negative image block.

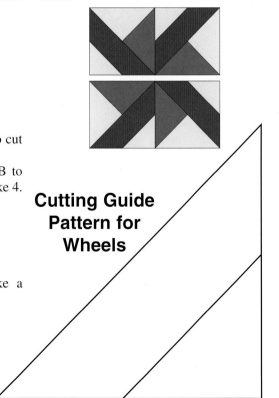

CUTTING
NOTE: *See "Cutting Tip for Wheels" on page 27.*
• Cut 1: 3 1/4" square, light, then cut it in quarters diagonally to yield 4 triangles
• Cut 1: 1 1/2" x 17" strip, same light
• Cut 1: 3 1/4" square, dark, then cut it in quarters diagonally to yield 4 triangles
• Cut 1: 1 1/2" x 17" strip, dark

DIRECTIONS
• Make a full-size cutting guide using the pattern provided. Mark the line on the cutting guide.
• Stitch a dark and a light triangle together along one short side to make Triangle A, as shown. Make 4.

• Stitch the 1 1/2" x 17" dark strip and the 1 1/2" x 17" light strip, right sides together along their length, to make a pieced strip.
• Place the strip right side up on a cutting

mat. Place the cutting guide on the strip, close to one end and aligning the marked line with the seam line.

• Cut along the edges of the guide to cut Triangle B from the strip. Cut 4.
• Stitch a Triangle A to a Triangle B to make a quarter-section, as shown. Make 4.

• Join two quarter-sections to make a half-block, as shown. Make 2.

• Join the half-blocks to complete the block.

Cutting Guide Pattern for Wheels

"X" is for X-Quartet

The X-Quartet has the distinction of being just one of three traditional blocks that begin with the letter "X." First published in the 1920s or 1930s, this block was known as X-Quartet in *Woman's World*, a Chicago periodical that also sold mail-order patterns. According to the *Encyclopedia of Pieced Quilt Patterns*, the block was called Double Quartet in *Capper's Weekly*, while the *Kansas City Star* named it Flying X.

Because the block is a lively one with lots of movement, you may wish to use sashing strips between blocks to quiet them in a multiblock quilt.

X-Quartet is a versatile block. Imagine it pieced in bright pastel prints from 1930s-style reproduction fabrics. Visualize it in Christmas prints or in red, white and blue for a patriotic look. Regardless of how you color the block, you'll find it easy to piece the no-template way.

CUTTING
- Cut 4: 1 7/8" squares, light
- Cut 4: 1 1/2" squares, same light
- Cut 4: 1 1/2" squares, medium
- Cut 4: 1 7/8" squares, dark

DIRECTIONS
- Use a pencil to mark a diagonal line from corner to corner on the wrong side of each 1 7/8" light square.
- Place a marked square on a 1 7/8" dark square, right sides together. Stitch 1/4" away from the diagonal line on both sides. Make 4.

- Cut the squares on the marked lines to yield 8 pieced squares.
- Lay out 4 pieced squares to form a pinwheel, as shown, and stitch them together.

- Stitch a 1 1/2" light square to each remaining pieced square to make a pieced rectangle, as shown. Make 4.

- Stitch 2 pieced rectangles to opposite sides of the pinwheel to form the center section.

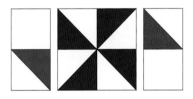

- Stitch a 1 1/2" medium square to each end of a remaining rectangle to make a pieced row, as shown. Make 2.

- Stitch the pieced rows to the remaining sides of the center section to complete the block.

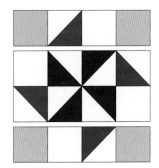

Cutting Tip for Wheels

If you plan to use directional fabrics like stripes, plaids or one-way prints in the wheels block, cut two squares from the print rather than one. That's because the stripes will run in two different directions when the squares are cut into triangles, as shown. One square yields two sets of matching triangles. You need four triangles that match, so cutting a second square into triangles will give you the number needed. Use the leftover set in another block or save it for another project.

"Y" is for Yankee Puzzle

Join four hour-glass units to make the Four-Patch Yankee Puzzle block. Although the design is composed of just one pattern piece, you won't even need a template to make the block.

Yankee Puzzle is one of the four-patch puzzle blocks identified in *Old Patchwork Quilts and the Women Who Made Them*. According to the author, "there are almost as many 'puzzle' patterns as there are 'stars'."

The term Yankee is a nickname that has evolved to refer to an ever-widening group of people. It is believed to have been used by Dutch settlers in New York to describe an inhabitant of New England in colonial times. During the Civil War, the term was used for an inhabitant of one of the northern or Union states. Today, it is used for an inhabitant of the United States.

The block was also published under other names. The *Encyclopedia of Pieced Quilt Patterns* indicates that several periodicals published by the *Kansas City Star* referred to the block as Hour Glass (1932), Envelope Quilt (1942) and The Whirling Blade (1944). Other popular pattern sources named the block Big Dipper (Ladies Art Company) and Bow Ties ("Nancy Cabot"). "Evangeline's," a 1930s pattern column in the St. John, New Brunswick, *Maritime Farmer*, called the design Pork and Beans.

Each block requires two 3 1/4" squares of light fabric and two of dark. However, by cutting the two dark squares from different fabrics and then combining them in the hour-glass units, you can emphasize the pinwheel formed at the block center.

The diagonal lines in the block give it direction and a lively feel. When joined side by side in a straight-set, the block is lost. You may find that sashing strips will help to quiet the design and retain a block focus. Have fun exploring the effects of color when you dig into your fabric scraps to find likely combinations for this easy-to-piece block.

CUTTING
- Cut 2: 3 1/4" squares, light
- Cut 2: 3 1/4" squares, dark

DIRECTIONS
- Draw diagonal lines from corner to corner on the wrong side of each light square.
- Place a marked square on a dark square, right sides together. Stitch 1/4" away from both sides of one diagonal line. Make 2.

- Cut only on the marked line between the stitching lines.
- Open the units and press the seam allowances toward the dark fabric, forming pieced squares.
- Place two pieced squares, right sides together, butting the seams and placing dark triangles against light ones. Extend the marked line to the corner of the dark triangle.

- Stitch 1/4" away from both sides of the marked line, as before. Cut on the marked line.

- Open the unit and press the seam allowance in either direction to make an hour-glass unit. Make 4.

- Lay out the units. Stitch the units into pairs and join the pairs to complete the block.

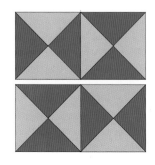

"Z" is for Z Block

According to the *Encyclopedia of Pieced Quilt Patterns*, the "Z" block was published in the early 1900s by the Ladies Art Company. Though it's an alphabet block, the design was unnamed when published.

Because the design is a realistic one, a straight set with sashing is a good choice to show off the blocks.

You'll note that we made a slight alteration to the original block and made it easy to piece using foundations. Stitch a single block to include in a sampler quilt or make several for a "Z Quilt."

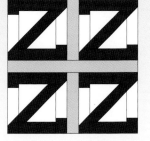

MATERIALS
- Scrap of one light and one dark print, each at least 8" square.
- Paper for the foundations

CUTTING
Fabric for foundation piecing will be cut as you stitch the block. Each piece should be 1/2" larger on all sides than the section it will cover. Refer to Stitching Tips *(page 32) as needed.*

DIRECTIONS
Follow the foundation-piecing instructions in Stitching Tips *to piece the block.*
- Trace the full-size patterns on the foundation paper, transferring all lines and numbers and leaving a 1" space between foundations. Make one Unit A and 2 Unit B's. Cut each one out 1/2" beyond the broken line.

For Unit A:
- Use the following fabrics in these positions:
  - 1 - dark print
  - 2, 3 - light print
  - 4, 5 - dark print

For each Unit B:
- Use the following fabrics in these positions:
  - 1 - light print
  - 2, 3 - dark print
- Baste each foundation in the seam allowance, halfway between the stitching line and the broken line, to hold the fabrics in place, if desired.

- Trim each foundation on the broken line.
- Stitch Unit B's to opposite sides of Unit A, as shown, to complete the block.

Foundation Patterns for Z Block

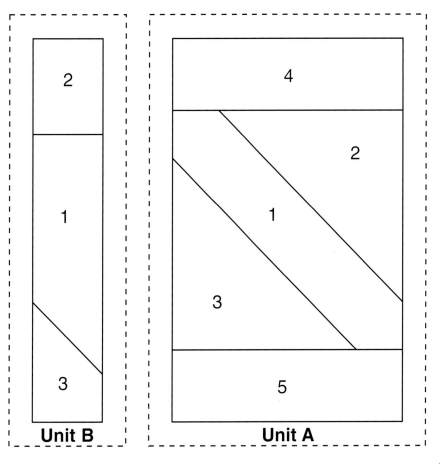

Unit B

Unit A

Mini Quilt Blocks
SAMPLER

Turn your little blocks into a lively sampler

Joyce placed her sampler blocks in A to Z order moving from left to right across the quilt. Place your blocks in any arrangement that pleases you. You may want to consider orienting the blocks horizontally (rather than vertically as they are shown here) if a horizontal quilt will better fit the space in which you wish to display it.

QUILT SIZE: 34 1/2" x 39 1/2"
BLOCK SIZE: 4" square

MATERIALS
Yardage is estimated for 44" fabric.
• Assorted blue prints, totaling 1/3 yard, for the cornerstones and border
• Assorted prints, totaling 3/4 yard, for the border and corner blocks
• 71 prints, each at least 2" x 4 1/2", for the sashing
• 1/3 yard tan stripe, for the sashing
• 1/4 yard blue print, for the binding
• 39" x 44" piece of backing fabric
• 39" x 44" piece of thin batting

DIRECTIONS
Make one of each block in the book to use in the quilt center. Instructions for the corner blocks, cornerstones, pieced sashings and border begin below. The pattern piece is full size and includes a 1/4" seam allowance, as do all dimensions given.

For the Cornerstones and Pieced Sashings:
• Cut 42: 1 1/2" squares, assorted blue prints
• Cut 2: 3/4" x 4 1/2" strips, from each of 71 prints
NOTE: *Joyce made 30 dark blue sashings and placed them around the outside edges of the quilt center and corner blocks. If you wish to do the same, cut 60 of your*

3/4" x 4 1/2" strips from assorted blue prints and refer to the quilt photo for sashing color placement.
• Cut 71: 1" x 4 1/2" strips, tan stripe
For the Border, Corner blocks and binding:
• Cut 26: 1 1/2" x 4 1/2" strips, assorted blue prints
• Cut 56: 1 1/2" x 4 1/2" strips, assorted prints
• Cut 32: 1 1/2" x 16" strips, assorted prints
• Cut 4: 1 3/4" x 44" strips, blue print, for the binding

DIRECTIONS
• Stitch four 1 1/2" x 16" assorted print strips together to make a pieced panel, as shown. Make 8.

• From each pieced panel cut a 4 1/2" square and two triangle A's, as shown. Label the squares Border Block A and set them aside.

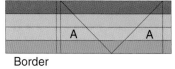

Border
Block A

• Stitch 2 triangle A's cut from 2 different panels together, to make a Corner Block, as shown. Make 8. Set them aside.

• Stitch a 1" x 4 1/2" tan stripe strip between two 3/4" x 4 1/2" same print strips to make a pieced sashing, as shown. Make 71.

• Referring to the quilt photo, lay out the pieced sashings, 4 Corner Blocks, the sampler blocks and the 1 1/2" blue print squares.
• Join six 1 1/2" blue print squares and 5 pieced sashings to make a sashing row, as shown. Make 7.

• Join 5 blocks and 6 pieced sashings to make a block row. Make 6.

• Stitch the sashing rows and block rows together to complete the quilt center.
• Stitch four 1 1/2" x 4 1/2" assorted print

strips together to make a Border Block B, as shown. Make 14.

• Lay the 1 1/2" x 4 1/2" blue print strips around the quilt center, so they are adjacent to blue cornerstones, as shown.

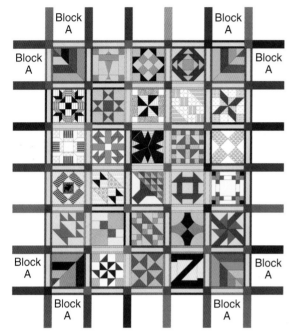

Block A Block A
Block A Block A
Block A Block A
Block A Block A

• Referring to the quilt photo and the assembly diagram, place the Border Block A's in the indicated spaces, carefully matching fabric color with the Corner Blocks.
• Referring to the quilt photo for directional placement, lay the remaining corner blocks in the corners of the quilt border.
• Fill in the rest of the spaces with the Border Block B's.
  • Join the blocks and blue print strips for the side borders and stitch them to the long sides of the quilt.
  • Join the blocks and blue print strips for the top and bottom borders and stitch them to the remaining sides of the quilt.
• Finish according to *Stitching Tips* (page 32) using the 1 3/4" x 44" blue print strips, for the binding.

A

Pattern for Mini Quilt Blocks Sampler

Historical Sources

As you read about the history of the traditional blocks presented in this book, you'll come across many sources for the original designs and historical information. You'll find that some of the blocks once appeared in the *Kansas City Star*, a regional daily newspaper. Others were offered by **The Ladies Art Company** of St. Louis, a mail order source for quilt patterns from the late 19th into the early 20th century, and the *Farm Journal*, a periodical begun in the 1800s that was a mail order source of quilt patterns. For more than 30 years, quilt patterns were a regular feature enjoyed by its many readers. Other early sources for some of the blocks include the "**Nancy Page Quilt Club**," a syndicated column which appeared in periodicals nationwide from the 1920s to the 1940s. The column was written by designer Florence LaGanke. **The McKim Studios**, based in Independence, Missouri, was yet another mail-order source for quilt patterns in the 1920s and 30s. *Farmer's Wife*, a periodical published in St. Paul, Minnesota, through the late 1930s, offered patterns too. The periodical eventually merged with *Farm Journal*. A syndicated column called "**Nancy Cabot**," written by Loretta Leitner Rising, appeared in the *Chicago Tribune*. Laura Wheeler designs were published by **Old Chelsea Station Needlecraft Service**, a New York mail-order pattern company established in the 1930s which also sold patterns under the designer names of Alice Brooks and Carol Curtis. Patterns by Louise Fowler Roote appeared in *Capper's Weekly*, a newspaper published in the 1920s. Aunt Martha was the most common designer name used for syndicated patterns by **Colonial Patterns** of Kansas City. Their patterns were also published under the designer names Aunt Ellen, Aunt Matilda and Betsy Ross. *Progressive Farmer* is a periodical that has been published in Birmingham, Alabama, since 1895. It has offered quilt patterns and booklets throughout its history. You'll find several of these historic pattern sources listed for many of the block designs.

References used for historical information include *The Romance of the Patchwork Quilt* by Carrie A. Hall and Rose G. Kretsinger (Dover Publications, 1985), first published in 1935; *Old Patchwork Quilts and the Women Who Made Them* by Ruth Finley (EPM, 1992), originally published in 1929; and the *Encyclopedia of Pieced Quilt Patterns, Vol. I* and *Encyclopedia of Pieced Quilt Patterns* (the American Quilters Society, 1993), both by Barbara Brackman.

Stitching Tips

MAKING THE BLOCKS:

Basic Information

All patterns in this book include 1/4" seam allowances. We recommend using 100% cotton to piece the blocks.

Templates

Trace pattern pieces onto clear plastic. Use a permanent marker to list the block name, pattern letter and grainline on each template. Some pattern pieces have dots to help with proper alignment before stitching. If the instructions call for an **R**, the template must be reversed before tracing to cut that pattern piece.

With the exception of the Z Block, which is foundation pieced, the solid line on all pattern pieces is the cutting line and the broken line is the sewing line.

For machine piecing, make the template with the seam allowances. Trace around the template on the right side of the fabric.

For hand piecing, make the template without the seam allowances. Trace the template on the wrong side of the fabric, flipping all directional (asymmetrical) templates before tracing, and add a 1/4" seam allowance as you cut the fabric pieces out.

Marking Fabric

We suggest using silver or white marking tools for dark fabrics and fine line pencils for light fabrics. Always use a sharp pencil and a light touch.

Hand Piecing

Use a thin, short needle ("sharp") to ensure a flat seam. Sew only on the marked sewing line using small, even stitches.

Machine Piecing

Set the stitch length to 14 stitches per inch. Cut a length of masking tape or moleskin foot pad about 1/4" x 2". Place a clear plastic ruler under and to the left of the needle aligning the right edge of the ruler 1/4" from the point of the needle along the throat plate. Stick the masking tape or moleskin in place at the ruler's edge. Feed fabric under the needle, touching this guide.

When directions call for you to start or stop stitching 1/4" from edges, as for set-in pieces, backstitch to secure the seam. Otherwise, stitch the pieces from edge to edge.

Pressing

Press seams toward the darker of the two fabrics, unless directed to do otherwise in the pattern. Press abutting seams in opposite directions whenever possible. Use a dry iron and press carefully using an up and down motion to avoid distorting the blocks.

Foundation Piecing

The Z block is foundation pieced. For each foundation, trace all of the lines and numbers onto paper. The solid lines are stitching lines and the broken line is the cutting line. The fabric pieces you select do not have to be cut precisely. Be generous when cutting the pieces as excess fabric will be trimmed away after sewing each seam. Your goal is to cut a piece that covers the numbered area and extends into surrounding areas after seams are stitched. Generally, fabric pieces should be large enough to extend 1/2" beyond the seamline on all sides before stitching. For sections without angles, 1/4" may be sufficient. Select a short stitch length, 14 stitches per inch.

Place fabric pieces on the unmarked side of the foundation and stitch on the marked side. Center the first piece, right side up, over section 1 on the unmarked side. Hold the foundation up to a light to make sure that the raw edges of the fabric extend beyond the seamline on all sides. Hold this first piece in place with a small dab of glue or a pin, if desired. Place the fabric for section 2 on the first piece, right sides together. Turn the foundation over and sew on the line between 1 and 2, extending the stitching past the beginning and end of the line by a few stitches on both ends. Trim the seam allowance to 1/8". Fold the section 2 piece back, right side up, and press. Continue adding pieces to the foundation in the same manner until all sections are covered and the block is complete.

To avoid disturbing stitches, it is best not to remove the paper until all of your blocks have been joined together and a border has been added to your quilt. The foundation paper will have been perforated by the stitching and can be gently pulled free. If necessary, use tweezers to carefully remove sections of the paper.

FINISHING YOUR QUILTS:

Cutting Setting and Corner Triangles

If you plan to set your 4" blocks on point, you'll need two sizes of triangles—one size for setting triangles and one size for the corners. It's easy to cut them from squares. To keep your quilt square and prevent stretching on the edges, it's important to place the bias edges of the triangles against the blocks and away from the edges of the quilt.

For setting triangles:

Cut a 7" square in quarters diagonally to make 4 setting triangles.

For corner Triangles:

Cut a 3 3/4" square in half diagonally to make 2 corner triangles.

Sashings

If you want to use sashings in your quilts, cut them the desired finished width plus 1/2" added for seam allowances. Cut sashings 4 1/2" long if they are to be stitched between blocks. To determine the length of sashings placed between rows, measure a completed row and cut the sashings that length.

Borders

To add borders to your completed quilt center, measure the length of the quilt. Cut 2 borders that length and the finished width you desire plus 1/2" added for seam allowances. Sew them to the long sides of the quilt. Measure the width of the quilt, including the borders. Cut 2 borders that length and the same width as before. Sew them to the remaining sides of the quilt.

Mitering Corners

Measure the length of your quilt top and add 2 times your determined border width plus 2". Cut border strips this measurement. Match the center of the quilt top with the center of the border strip and pin to the corners. Stitch each border to the quilt top beginning, ending and backstitching each seamline 1/4" from the edge of the quilt top. After all

borders have been attached in this manner, miter one corner at a time. With the quilt top lying right side down, lay one border over the other. Draw a straight line at a 45° angle from the inner corner to the outer corner, as shown.

Reverse the positions of the borders and mark another straight line from corner to corner, in the same manner.

Place the borders, right sides together, with marked seamlines carefully matched and pinned and stitch from the outer edge to the inner corner, backstitching at the inner corner. Open the mitered seam to make sure it lies flat, trim excess fabric and press.

Layer your quilt with batting and backing and quilt as desired.

Binding

For straight-edged quilts, a double-fold French binding is an attractive, durable and easy finish. NOTE: *If your quilt has curved edges, binding strips must be cut on the bias.* To make 1/4" finished binding, cut each strip 1 3/4" wide. Sew binding strips together with diagonal seams; trim and press seams open.

Fold the binding strip in half lengthwise, wrong side in, and press. Position the folded binding strip on the right side of the quilt top, aligning the raw edges of the binding with the edge of the quilt top. Leave approximately 4" of the binding strip free. Beginning several inches from one corner of the quilt, stitch the binding to the quilt with a 1/4" seam allowance. When you reach a corner, stop stitching exactly 1/4" from the edge. Backstitch, clip threads and remove the quilt from the machine. Fold the binding up and away, creating a 45° angle, as shown.

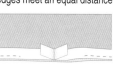

Fold the binding down, as shown, and begin stitching at the edge.

Continue stitching around the quilt to within 4" of the starting point. To finish, fold both strips back along the edge of the quilt so that the folded edges meet an equal distance from both lines of stitching and the binding lies flat on the quilt. Finger press to crease the folds. Cut both strips 7/8" beyond the folds.

Open both strips and place the ends at right angles to each other, right sides together. Fold the bulk of the quilt out of your way. Join the strips with a diagonal seam, as shown.

Trim the seam to 1/4" and press it open. Refold the joined strip, wrong side in. Place the binding flat against the quilt and finish stitching it to the quilt. Trim the batting and backing even with the edge of the quilt top so that the binding will be filled with batting when you fold the binding to the back of the quilt. Blindstitch the binding to the back of the quilt, covering the seamline.

Sign and date your quilt.